Mrs. Claus
RUNS AMOK!
(A LOVE STORY)

Written and Illustrated by

SHIRLEY MAXINE CLAUS

M
ax ™

MRS. CLAUS RUNS AMOK!
(A LOVE STORY)

by Shirley Maxine Claus

© 2023 Max Paige LLC, Milwaukee Wisconsin USA

ISBN 978-0-9979078-9-6

For Hel,
the Center of My Universe

Wouldn't it be magical
to live with Santa at the
North Pole?

Think of the fun you'd
have with those cute little elves
and adorable reindeer.

Just imagine those
lovely snowflakes floating
gently to the ground...
all day, every day.

It's the definition of
joy, right?

Nothing to do except cook a few meals and take loving care of your man... an immortal giant elf with rosy-red cheeks and a very long white beard.

Umm... why *are* those cheeks so rosy?

And those elves... they all seem to have beards. Aren't there any female elves around? And who cleans up after all those reindeer? I'll bet it's a hot day at the North Pole before MISTER Santa Claus shovels out a reindeer stall.

That Mrs. Claus must be one patient woman... and an excellent barista. Those elves probably need the extra caffeine as much as she does.

IMAGINE the pressures of living in a secret Arctic compound with several hundred picky elves and twelve arrogant reindeer (so they can fly... whatever).

No visitors, no phone calls, and all the mail is written in crayon. Now, add a husband who does nothing but make toys — all day, every day — just so he can give them away. How do you run a household like that?? And balancing the checking account? Forget it.

This is the wretched plight of Mrs. Santa Claus. All year long, day after numbing day, she mends tiny elf socks and cooks tiny elf meals, serving them on tiny elf plates, and for what? A great big "Ho-Ho-Ho!" is about as good as it gets for a girl stuck at the top of the world without cable.

Unlike everyone else at the North Pole, Mrs. Claus is only human, and come December she is tethered to sanity with a loose knot. In quiet desperation, she waits for her annual night off — Christmas Eve. It's the one night of the year when her man is far, far away. The one night when she has no responsibility whatsoever.

But this year something is amiss. This year, Mrs. Claus is beyond a good book. She's beyond a warm comforter and a nice cup of cocoa. Way beyond.

Nothing too serious mind you. Nothing you couldn't mend with a sip or two of chardonnay, but nonetheless difficult to explain when Santa returns home, because this Christmas Eve...

Mrs. Claus runs amok!™

"Bye-bye, Sweetheart.
Fly safely."

"Never fear, my love!
I'll be back before you know it!"

"No rush! I'll find something
to busy myself with."

"Ho-Ho-Ho!"

The equestrian arts
bring out Mrs. Claus' natural
competitive spirit.

Mrs. Claus understands
the importance of exercise,
and is not afraid to engage in
traditionally male sports.

Like many women,
Mrs. Claus uses gardening to
help relieve the stress of today's
fast-paced lifestyle.

Mealtime often brings unique challenges for a woman like Mrs. Claus.

Mrs. Claus takes advantage of the ready availability of toys at the North Pole.

The lack of
elf-scale dental floss at the
North Pole is a constant worry
for Mrs. Claus.

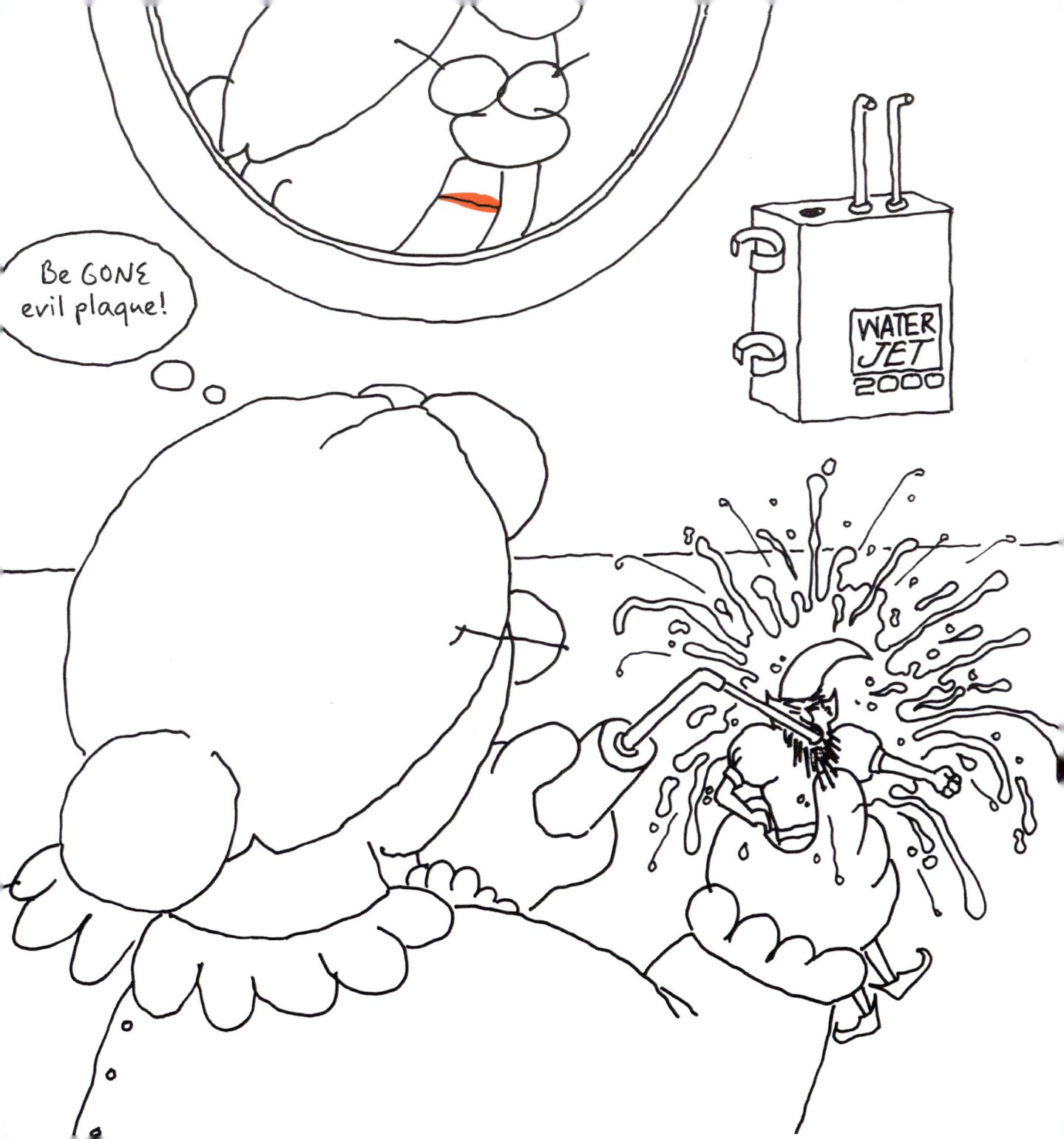

Mrs. Claus isn't a social media girl. But despite the weak signal at the North Pole, she still manages to connect on the important stuff.

It had been a long day...
for everybody.

It's past midnight and
still no word...

And then...

An exhausted
Santa fills the last stocking
on his journey... the most
important one of all.

"I missed you SO MUCH!!!"

"Me too! What did you do
while I was gone?"

"Nothing much. A little gardening,
some cooking, exercise. You know...
same old, same old."

"Okay! Well... I'm beat.
Think I'm gonna hit the sack."

"Umm... I'm thinkin' you could stay up just a little longer maybe?"

"I dunno Hon... it's been a long night. I really need some sleep."

"What you need Mr. Claus, is another big hug. How 'bout I turn off this light?"

"Ho-Ho-HOOOOO!"

GLOSSARY

ELVES (Core Population) – Immortal beings, 100% male, generally resembling humans but only 18 to 24 inches tall. Hard-working beings that are particularly adept at toymaking. Scientists generally agree that the only remaining population of Elves is at the North Pole. That said, Elves are very resourceful creatures, and may be concealing their presence at other locations on planet Earth. They are said to be fluent in all known languages, but speak with an Eastern European accent. The origin of Elves is unknown. Estimates of their numbers range from 200 - 400.

GIANT ELVES – Immortal beings, indistinguishable from humans, 60 to 72 inches tall. Until recently, it was assumed there was only one Giant Elf on Earth: Santa Claus. But in the winter of 2023, another Giant Elf stepped forward to reveal herself: Ms. Shirley Maxine Claus of International Falls, Minnesota USA. Shirley Claus is the sister of Santa Claus, and formerly resided at the North Pole with her brother, where she provided all support services for Mr. Claus and the Elves. Shirley claims to be the last remaining female Giant Elf. She is also known by her nickname, "Max".

MRS. SANTA CLAUS (Original name unknown) – Human female, approx. 55 years of age, standing 5'-1" tall, weighing approximately 170 pounds. According to Shirley Claus, Mrs. Claus met Santa around midnight at an all-night diner somewhere in Kansas. Santa was near exhaustion and desperate for a strong cup of coffee. Single and without living family, Mrs. Claus was the late-night manager and lone employee on duty. Recognizing the importance of the situation, she made a fresh pot of coffee, turned out the lights and locked the doors. They talked for over an hour before Santa declared he must get back to work. But before he left, they agreed to meet again... same time next year. When year three came, Santa arrived with a heavy wool coat for the future Mrs. Claus, and a proposal of marriage. She wrote a kind note to her boss and never returned.

NORTH POLE – Reportedly, the North Pole (or somewhere near it) is the headquarters of Santa Claus' operations. Though all literature regarding the "Jolly Old Elf" refers to the North Pole as Santa's residence, scientists have thus far been unsuccessful in their attempts to find his compound. Despite extensive satellite surveillance and fly-overs, the exact location has yet to be identified. The United States Postal Service, along with similar organizations all around the world, steadfastly refuse to reveal how and where they deliver mail to Mr. Claus.

NORTH POLE REINDEER – Generally indistinguishable from southern reindeer, North Pole Reindeer are immortal… and they can fly. They use the power of flight to transport Santa and his sleigh around the world. Given their lack of wings, scientists have been unable to explain this remarkable ability. Some have speculated they are from another planet, and possess intelligence and stamina far greater than Earthly species. There are believed to be at least nine reindeer in Santa's stable: Dasher, Dancer, Prancer, Vixen, Comet, Cupid, Donner, Blitzen, and Rudolph. Though never observed by any living human, literature claims that Rudolph's nose glows bright red – enabling Santa's sleigh to navigate through a variety of nighttime weather conditions.

SLEIGH – Santa's only means of transportation, the sleigh is designed to navigate any terrain, with particular attention to snow-covered rooftops. Though Santa usually travels alone, the sleigh measures about 6' x 12' and will easily seat two. The sleigh is powered by flying reindeer capable of pulling the sleigh through the air or on the ground. The rear portion of Santa's sleigh is reserved for a large bag of gifts. Scientists have concluded that the storage area on the sleigh is wholly inadequate to accommodate the volume of gifts necessary to fulfill the requests from millions of children. This incongruity has led to speculation that Santa maintains a complex network of storage facilities all around the globe. A prominent science writer for the New York Times has promoted a hypothesis that is gaining traction with many. They postulate, "Even an immortal Giant Elf with seemingly unlimited resources would have difficulty managing and maintaining such a distribution network. There must be others involved. Santa must have a helper we don't know about." After providing a great many math-based arguments, they continue: "Logic dictates that Santa's distribution network must operate anonymously year-round, if for no other reason than to avoid detection. Only one such network exists in the world. It is owned by a man of enormous wealth and power. A man who likes to stay out of the news and protects his privacy with great care." This multi-billionaire has been contacted by the science editor of a leading New York newspaper, along with a great many scientists and news organizations. His answer is always the same: "No Comment." Worthy of note: this well-known organization only closes its warehouses one day a year – Christmas Day, begging the question, "Is this billionaire actually a Giant Elf? Perhaps even Santa's brother??" Only Santa and the author of this book know for sure.

Me on date night   Shirley Claus

www.ingramcontent.com/pod-product-compliance
Lightning Source LLC
Chambersburg PA
CBRC100735150426
42811CB00069B/1897